T0318142

Cover
Tama Art University Library
(Hachioji Campus)
Toyo Ito & Associates Architects
photo Ishiguro Photographic Institute

Project Coordination
Rosi Guadagno and Patrizia Vicenzi

Graphic
R.A.D.L.&

Photo
© Hedrich Blessing / OWPP, pp. 113, 114
Peter Berson, pp. 8, 50, 52
Federico Brunetti, p. 49
Mario Carrieri, pp. 88, 222
Alberto Cocchi, p. 252
Peter Forgensen, p. 154
Jens Hauspurg, p. 232
Saverio Lombardi Vallauri, pp. 131, 132
Jan Malý, pp. 64, 66
André Morin, p. 238
Mikkel Mortensen, pp. 23, 24
Andrés Otero, p. 124
Antonio Pedrosa, pp. 99, 100, 109, 110
Laura Rizzi, pp. 166, 168
Ivan Sarfatti, pp. 103, 104, 106, 141, 142,
144, 146, 149, 150, 200, 202, 204, 225,
226, 228, 230, 259, 260, 262, 264, 266
Filip Šlapal, pp. 79, 80, 82
Luca Tamburlini, pp. 300, 302
John Van Groenedaal, pp. 291, 292, 295,
296, 298
Peter Wurmli, p. 34
Ishiguro Photographic Institute, pp. 15, 16

Special Thanks
Minako Morita
Nihan Simsek
Peter Smrek
Smussen.com
Unifor
Well-adv

First published in Italy in 2009 by
Skira Editore S.p.A.
Palazzo Casati Stampa
via Torino 61
20123 Milano
Italy
www.skira.net

© 2008 by Luceplan spa, Milano
© 2008 Design.doc for the texts
© 2008 Skira editore
All rights reserved

Printed and bound in Italy. First edition

ISBN: 978-88-572-0023-1

Distributed in North America by Rizzoli
International Publications, Inc.,
300 Park Avenue South, New York,
NY 10010, USA.
Distributed elsewhere in the world
by Thames and Hudson Ltd.,
181A High Holborn, London WC1V 7QX,
United Kingdom.

LUCEPLAN WORLDWIDE

SKIRA

nautica
SHIPS

allestimenti temporanei
TEMPORARY EXHIBITIONS

spazi commerciali
COMMERCIAL SPACES

UFFICI
OFFICES

HOTEL e ristoranti
HOTELS and restaurants

SPAZI PUBBLICI
PUBLIC spaces

paesi
countries

◑ Dal 1978 un percorso di creatività industriale che vanta svariati premi e importanti riconoscimenti, ma soprattutto la presenza con i propri prodotti in decine di realizzazioni, importante prova della validità dei risultati. Luoghi di lavoro, di studio, di incontro, più generalmente di vita quotidiana, in cui le utilities di Luceplan e di Elementi di Luceplan – sistemi di illuminazione per l'architettura dedicati al mondo del progetto e del contract – svolgono i servizi per i quali sono stati ideati, dando nel contempo carattere allo spazio.

Un paesaggio eterogeneo di opere di architettura italiane e straniere, di ampia e di ridotta estensione, firmate da progettisti affermati e da giovani promesse, in cui la cultura tecnica e umanistica dell'azienda, con la "classicità contemporanea e innovativa" dei suoi prodotti, diventa protagonista, componente che segna la qualità di ogni realizzazione. Punti focali di tutte le fotografie raccolte in questo volume – nel loro insieme interpretabili anche come abaco di possibilità, di potenzialità –, le collezioni Luceplan e Elementi di Luceplan si raccontano da sole, mostrando scenari estetici e di luce che non hanno bisogno di parole.

Un racconto quindi solo per immagini. Non mero catalogo né vero e proprio libro, forse più una sorta di "album di luoghi e di flussi luminosi": tante istantanee da tutto il mondo per catturare quello che solitamente non si conosce, ovvero la vita reale delle collezioni Luceplan dopo la ricerca, la produzione, la vendita, nel mondo globale.

✳ Since 1978, a shining example of industrial creativity that has received a series of awards and other important marks of recognition, but above all seen its products included in dozens of interior designs, in an important demonstration of the validity of its results. Places of work, study, meeting and, more in general, daily life, in which the "utilities" of Luceplan and Elementi di Luceplan – lighting systems for architecture dedicated to the world of design and contract supply – perform the functions for which they have been conceived, while giving character to the space.

A varied panorama of Italian and foreign works of architecture, on a large and small scale, created by established designers and promising youngsters, in which the company's technical and artistic culture, with the "contemporary and innovative classicism" of its products, play a leading role, as components that set the seal of quality on every project. Focal points of all the photographs in this volume – which taken as a whole can also be seen as a gamut of possibilities, of potentialities – the Luceplan and Elementi di Luceplan collections speak for themselves, showing us settings in which the aesthetic quality of the lighting has no need of words.

So it is a story told exclusively in pictures. Neither just a catalogue nor a book in the proper sense, it can perhaps best be described as a sort of "album of locations and streams of light": so many snapshots from all over the world capturing something to which we are not usually exposed, the real life of the Luceplan collections after research, production and sale, as they can be found the world over.

● Seit 1978 sind wir auf der Suche nach industrieller Kreativität, die mit zahlreichen Preisen und bedeutenden Anerkennungen ausgezeichnet wurde. Jedoch vor allem die Präsenz unserer Produkte in unzähligen Realisierungen ist ein sichtbarer Beweis für die Hochwertigkeit der erzielten Ergebnisse. Räume, die zum Arbeiten, Lernen oder zur Begegnung dienen, also einfach Orte des täglichen Lebens, in denen die utilities von Luceplan und Elementi di Luceplan – Beleuchtungssysteme für die Architektur der Projekt- und Contract-Bereiche – die ihnen zugedachten Funktionen erfüllen und gleichzeitig zur Charakterisierung des Raumes dienen.

Eine heterogene Landschaft von italienischen und ausländischen Werken großer und kleinerer Ausmaße, konzipiert von bekannten Designern mit großen Namen oder unbekannten aber vielversprechenden jungen Talenten, bei denen die technische und humanistische Kultur unseres Unternehmens in den Mittelpunkt gerückt und die „zeitgenössische und innovative Klassik" unserer Produkte als Ausdruck der Qualität in allen Realisierungen deutlich werden. Alle in diesem Band gesammelten Fotografien, in deren Brennpunkt die Kollektionen Luceplan und Elementi di Luceplan stehen und die in ihrer Gesamtheit auch als Werkzeug zur Darstellung der Möglichkeiten und Potentialitäten betrachtet werden können, sind selbstredend. Sie zeigen ästhetische und lichtgestalterische Szenarien, die keiner Worte bedürfen.

Eine Erzählung also, die nur aus Bildern besteht. Mehr als ein Katalog, ist dieses fast schon „Buch" eine Art „Album der Örtlichkeiten und Lichtströme": viele Schnappschüsse aus allen Teilen der Welt, um festzuhalten und zu zeigen was man normalerweise nicht kennt. Das wirkliche Leben der Luceplan-Kollektionen nach der Planung, der Produktion und dem Verkauf in der globalisierten Welt.

◖ Un parcours de création industrielle qui, depuis 1978, peut se targuer de nombreux prix et d'importantes récompenses, mais surtout de l'utilisation de ses produits dans de nombreuses réalisations, ce qui constitue la preuve irréfutable de la validité des résultats obtenus. Des espaces de travail, d'études, de rencontres, plus génériquement des lieux de vie quotidienne, où les productions Luceplan et Elementi di Luceplan – systèmes d'éclairage pour l'architecture destinés au monde des concepteurs et des entreprises spécialisées – rendent pleinement les services pour lesquels elles ont été pensées, tout en conférant du caractère à l'espace.

Un paysage hétérogène de créations architecturales, italiennes et étrangères, de dimensions contenues ou imposantes, portant la signature de concepteurs affirmés et de jeunes promesses, où la culture technique et humaniste de l'entreprise, associée au "classique tout contemporain et innovateur" de ses produits, devient protagoniste et dont les éléments caractérisent la qualité de chaque réalisation. Au centre de toutes les photographies rassemblées dans ce volume – globalement interprétables également comme une multitude de possibilités, de potentialités –, les collections Luceplan et Elementi di Luceplan parlent d'elles-mêmes et proposent des scénarios esthétiques et lumineux qui n'ont pas besoin d'être commentés.

Un récit, donc, composé uniquement d'images. Pas un simple catalogue, ni même un livre à proprement parler : peut-être plutôt une sorte "d'album de lieux et de flux lumineux", une kyrielle d'instantanés du monde entier pour capturer ce que, habituellement, l'on ne connaît pas, c'est-à-dire la vie réelle des collections Luceplan après les phases de recherche, de production, de commercialisation, dans le monde global.

◓ Un itinerario de creatividad industrial galardonado, desde el año 1978, con diversos premios e importantes reconocimientos y, sobre todo, con la presencia de sus propios productos en decenas de realizaciones: una prueba importante de la validez de los éxitos conseguidos. Lugares de trabajo, de estudio, de encuentro, en general de vida diaria, donde las utilities de Luceplan y Elementos de Luceplan – sistemas de iluminación para la arquitectura dedicados al mundo del proyecto y del contract – ofrecen los servicios que han inspirado su creación, proporcionando al mismo tiempo carácter al espacio.

Un paisaje heterogéneo de obras de arquitectura italianas y extranjeras, de amplia y de reducida extensión, firmadas por proyectistas famosos y por jóvenes promesas, donde la cultura técnica y humanística de la empresa, junto con "el mundo clásico contemporáneo e innovador" de sus productos, se convierten en protagonistas, en componentes que marcan la calidad de cada realización. Las colecciones Luceplan y Elementos de Luceplan, puntos focales de todas las fotografías reunidas en este volumen (interpretables conjuntamente también como ábaco de posibilidades y capacidades), se explican solas, mostrando escenarios estéticos y de luz que no necesitan comentarios.

Así pues, un relato que utiliza sólo las imágenes. No un simple catálogo ni propiamente un libro, quizá más una especie de "álbum de lugares y de flujos luminosos": muchas fotografías instantáneas de todo el mundo para capturar lo que normalmente no se conoce, es decir, la vida real de las colecciones Luceplan después de la búsqueda, la producción y la venta en el mundo global.

Tama University, *Tokyo*
Toyo Ito & Associates
Costanza

Tama University, *Tokyo*
Toyo Ito & Associates
Costanza

Ekol Lojistik, *Istanbul*
Tribunn Architectural
Aircon

Ekol Lojistik, *Istanbul*
Tribunn Architectural
Bap

Norden Shipping, *Copenhagen*
Dissing+Weitling
Berenice

Norden Shipping, *Copenhagen*
Dissing+Weitling
Berenice

Carris Public Transportation, *Lisbon*
Paula Moura, Miguel Arruda
Blow

Carris Public Transportation, *Lisbon*
Paula Moura, Miguel Arruda
Blow

St. Simon's Church, *Glasgow*
Foto-ma lighting architects and designers
e04 suspension Elementi di Luceplan

Amagerbanken, *Hellerup*
Christian Lund
Trama

Google EMEA Engineering Hub, *Zürich*
Camenzind Evolution
Titania

Wall AG, *Duiven*
ION Berlin - Carlo Ferrante
Orchestra

Wall AG, *Duiven*
ION Berlin - Carlo Ferrante
Orchestra

Wall AG, *Duiven*
ION Berlin - Carlo Ferrante
Orchestra

Allianz Teatro, *Assago*
A.G. Cavalchini, F. Librizzi
Costanza, Mix

Allianz Teatro, *Assago*
A.G. Cavalchini, F. Librizzi
Costanza, Mix

La biglietteria del teatro apre
due ore prima dell'inizio
degli spettacoli.
Al di fuori di tali orari è
possibile acquistare i biglietti
presso la biglietteria situata
all'ingresso principale del
DATCHFORUM

Allianz Teatro, *Assago*
A.G. Cavalchini, F. Librizzi
Costanza, Mix

Riccardo Beyerle, *Milano*
Urb A.M.
Strip

The New York Times, *New York*
Renzo Piano Building Workshop

The New York Times, *New York*
Renzo Piano Building Workshop
Berenice LED

Bon Marché Department Store, *Paris*
Technical Department of Bon Marché
Costanza

Bon Marché Department Store, *Paris*
Technical Department of Bon Marché
Glassglass

Bon Marché Department Store, *Paris*
Technical Department of Bon Marché
Costanza

Artic Palacio de Hielo, *Pamplona*
Pagola Illuminacion
Queen Titania

Tom Tom Suites, *Istanbul*
Pamir Architectural
Mirandolina

Blue Orange, *Praha*
Plan Architects, s.r.o.
Costanza

Blue Orange, *Praha*
Plan Architects, s.r.o.
Costanza

Gorton Monastery, *Manchester*
Austin Smith Lord
Consultant Engineers - RW Gregory
Glassglass

Gorton Monastery, *Manchester*
Austin Smith Lord
Consultant Engineers - RW Gregory
Glassglass

Samsung, Fuori Salone 2008, *Milano*
Isacco Brioschi
Mirandolina, Costanza

uscita di sicurezza
divieto di sosta

Samsung, Fuori Salone 2008, *Milano*
Isacco Brioschi
Pod lens

University of Dundee, *Dundee*
James F. Stephen Architects
Happy Happy

University Campus, *Brno*
A Plus Brno, a.s.
Fortebraccio

University Campus, *Brno*
A Plus Brno, a.s.
Zeno Elementi di Luceplan

University Campus, *Brno*
A Plus Brno, a.s.
Zeno Elementi di Luceplan

Circolo Filologico Milanese, *Milano*
Sergio Stocco
Costanza, Grande Costanza

Circolo Filologico Milanese, *Milano*
Sergio Stocco
Costanza, Grande Costanza

Novartis Pharma, *Basel*
Hannes Wettstein
Fortebraccio

Land Rover Showroom, *Ragusa*
Vittorio Battaglia, Home Line
Zeno Elementi di Luceplan

University of Amsterdam, *Amsterdam*

Blow

Teatro Strehler, *Milano*
Marco Zanuso
Piccolo Teatro (custom-made)

Teatro Strehler, *Milano*
Marco Zanuso
Piccolo Teatro (custom-made)

FC Porto Dragon House, *Porto*
Mario Azevedo - INAIN
Happy Happy

FC Porto Dragon House, *Porto*
Mario Azevedo - INAIN
Fortebraccio

Musée d'Orsay, *Paris*
Gae Aulenti
Glassglass

La Société des Amis
du Musée d'Orsay

Musée d'Orsay, *Paris*
Gae Aulenti
Costanza

Musée d'Orsay, *Paris*
Gae Aulenti
Costanza

Place Health Club, *Porto*
Mario Azevedo - INAIN
Metropoli

Place Health Club, *Porto*
Mario Azevedo - INAIN
Blow

Toshiba, *Chicago*
OWP/P
Pod lens

Toshiba, *Chicago*
OWP/P
Pod lens

Café Dagnis, *Malmö*
White Arch.
Grande Costanza

Fondation Cartier, *Paris*
Jean Nouvel
Costanza

Fondation Cartier, *Paris*
Jean Nouvel
Costanza

Fondation Cartier, *Paris*
Jean Nouvel
Costanza

Green Energy Design 2008, *Milano*
Matteo Vercelloni
Sky

Brasserie de l'Ouest, *Lyon*
Boucharlat
Titania

Brasserie de l'Ouest, *Lyon*
Boucharlat
Pod Lens

Fiera Milano, *Rho-Pero*
Massimiliano Fuksas
Zeno Elementi di Luceplan

Fiera Milano, *Rho-Pero*
Massimiliano Fuksas
Queen Titania

KDY Royal Danish Yacht Club, *Hellerup*
Vilhelm Lauritzen
Costanza

Istituto Clinico Humanitas, *Rozzano*
Ilaria dell'Acqua - Franco Raggi
Lightdisc

DR Byen, *Copenhagen*
PLH Architects
Fortebraccio

DR Byen, *Copenhagen*
PLH Architects
Fortebraccio

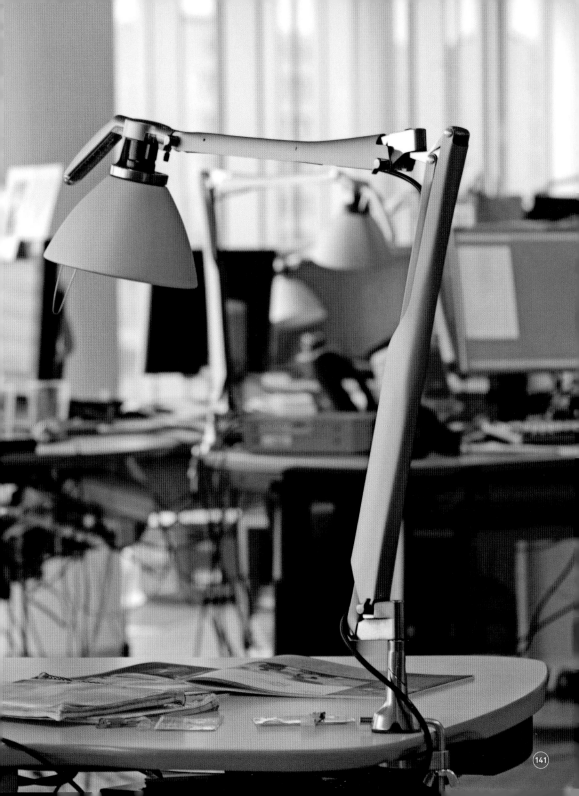

DR Byen, *Copenhagen*
PLH Architects
Grande Costanza

MSC Orchestra
De Jorio International Design

MSC Orchestra
De Jorio International Design
(custom-made)

Biblioteca Auris, *Vignola*
Paola Vidulli - Space Planning
Mix

Biblioteca Auris, *Vignola*
Paola Vidulli - Space Planning
Mix

Gästehaus im Apfelgarten, *Hoherbercha*
Michael Deppisch
Costanza, Costanzina

Copenhagen Island, *Copenhagen*
Kim Utzon Architects
Costanzina

Discovery 5 TV Network, *Paris*
Sébastien Dauge
Happy Happy

Discovery 5 TV Network, *Paris*
Sébastien Dauge
Supergiù

Hallenbad Zwettl fitness centre, *Zwettl*
Peter Staska, Buero CPM
Lightdisc

Design on Board 2008, *Bologna*
Talocci Design
Costanza, Costanzina

Design on Board 2008, *Bologna*
Talocci Design
Titania

Ferretti Altura 690, *Forli*

Costanzina

Ferretti 510, *Forli*

Costanzina

Mediapason TV Network, *Milano*
Euromilano / Alberto Catalano

Mediapason TV Network, *Milano*
Euromilano / Alberto Catalano
Glassglass

Mediapason TV Network, *Milano*
Euromilano / Alberto Catalano
Aircon, e02 Elementi di Luceplan

Mediapason TV Network, *Milano*
Euromilano / Alberto Catalano
Strip

Mediapason TV Network, *Milano*
Euromilano / Alberto Catalano
Metropoli, e02 Elementi di Luceplan

Mediapason TV Network, *Milano*
Euromilano / Alberto Catalano
Sky

Mediapason TV Network, *Milano*
Euromilano / Alberto Catalano
Sky

Democratic Department Shop, *Milano*
Paolo Giacopelli
Chichibio

Giellesse, Salone 2008, *Milano*
Massimo Colombo
d7

CISA Andrea Palladio, *Vicenza*
Alessandro Scandurra
Lightdisc, Fortebraccio

Samas, *Houten*
Inbo Architecten
Glassglass

Samas, *Houten*
Inbo Architecten
Costanza

Princess Cruises, *Monfalcone*
Gerolamo Scorza
Metropoli

Griffins Cafe, *Manchester*
ILS Client - RG Design
Glassglass

Griffins Cafe, *Manchester*
ILS Client - RG Design
Glassglass

Showroom Basketball Champion, *Bologna*
Jacopo Acciaro, Voltaire
(custom-made) Elementi di Luceplan

Showroom Basketball Champion , *Bologna*
Jacopo Acciaro, Voltaire
(custom-made) Elementi di Luceplan

Showroom Basketball Champion , *Bologna*
Jacopo Acciaro, Voltaire
(custom-made) Elementi di Luceplan

I Guess PCM, *Amsterdam*
Heyligers Design + Projects

I Guess PCM, *Amsterdam*
Heyligers Design + Projects
Agave

I Guess PCM, *Amsterdam*
Heyligers Design + Projects
Queen Titania

Café Zezé, *Copenhagen*
Maria Berntsen
Miranda

Café Zezé, *Copenhagen*
Maria Berntsen
Miranda

Valcucine, Fuori Salone 2008, *Milano*
Gabriele Centazzo
Queen Titania

Valcucine, Fuori Salone 2008, *Milano*
Gabriele Centazzo
Queen Titania

Musée du Quai Branly, *Paris*
Jean Nouvel, Gilles Clément
Costanza

Musée du Quai Branly, *Paris*
Jean Nouvel, Gilles Clément
Costanza

Wonsild & Søn, *Copenhagen*

Mirandolina, Costanza

Wonsild & Søn, *Copenhagen*

Miranda

Wonsild & Søn, *Copenhagen*

Costanza

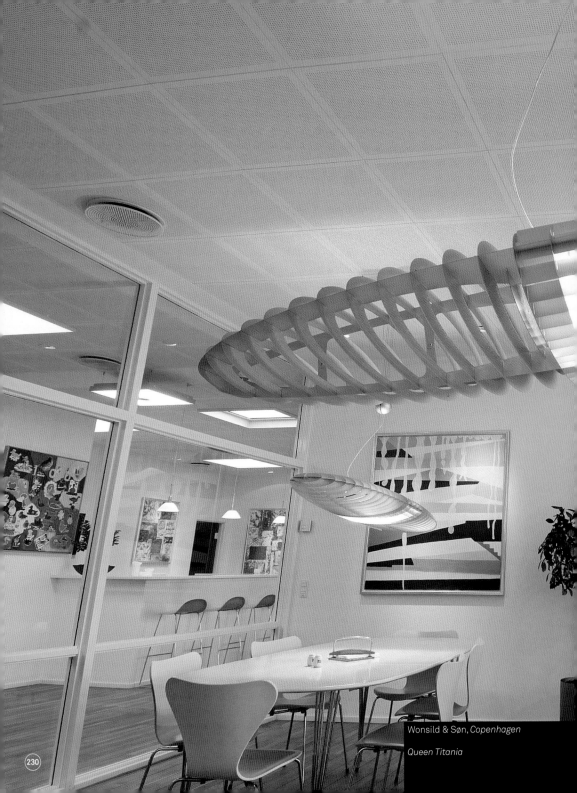

Wonsild & Søn, *Copenhagen*

Queen Titania

Bauhaus Universität, *Weimar*
Meck Architekten
Bap

Eclettis Headquarters, *Jesi*
Studio Schiavoni
e03, e01 square, a01 Elementi di Luceplan

Audi Porsche Showroom, *Marbella*
Hans-Jürgen Mehl
Zeno Elementi di Luceplan

Médiathèque, *Vénissieux*
Dominique Perrault
Costanzina

Kinderdagverblijf, *The Hague*
A70
Goggle, Aircon, Pod lens

meterkast

Helene Elsass Center, *Charlottenlund*

Costanza

Helene Elsass Center, *Charlottenlund*

Costanza

Health City fitness centre, *The Hague*

Agave

Health City fitness centre, *The Hague*

Agave

Health City fitness centre, *The Hague*

Agave, Titania

Riva 68' Ego Super, *La Spezia*

Costanzina

Shopping Centre, *Monza*
Immobiliare Europea / Corrado Rossetti
Sky solar version (custom-made)

Shopping Centre, *Monza*
Immobiliare Europea / Corrado Rossetti
Sky solar version (custom-made)

NNE Pharmaplan, *Søborg*
PLH Arch. Bine Solberg
Zeno Elementi di Luceplan

NNE Pharmaplan, *Søborg*
PLH Arch. Bine Solberg
Zeno Elementi di Luceplan

NNE Pharmaplan, *Søborg*
PLH Arch. Bine Solberg
Costanzina (custom-made)

NNE Pharmaplan, *Søborg*
PLH Arch. Bine Solberg
Aircon

NNE Pharmaplan, *Søborg*
PLH Arch. Bine Solberg
Berenice

Salone dell'Automobile 2007, *Ginevra*

Pod lens

Anne Frank Museum, *Amsterdam*

Anne Frank Museum, *Amsterdam*

Metropoli

Anne Frank Museum, *Amsterdam*

Metropoli

My Sushi, *Milano*

Pod lens

Zucchi, Centro Commerciale Sarca, *Milano*

Costanza

Peugeot Showroom, *Madrid*

Costanza

Marex spa, *Correggio*
Paolo Rizzatto
Lightdisc, Queen Titania (custom-made)

Marex spa, *Correggio*
Paolo Rizzatto
Zeno Elementi di Luceplan

Fleiner Möbel, *Stuttgart*

e01 square, a01 Elementi di Luceplan

Fleiner Möbel, *Stuttgart*

e01 square, a01 Elementi di Luceplan

Biermans Interieur, *Breda*

e01 square Elementi di Luceplan

Biermans Interieur, *Breda*

e01 square Elementi di Luceplan

Biermans Interieur, *Breda*

e04 suspension Elementi di Luceplan,
e01 square Elementi di Luceplan, Goggle

Biermans Interieur, *Breda*

e01 square Elementi di Luceplan

Biermans Interieur, *Breda*

e01 square Elementi di Luceplan

Nuova Accademia Belle Arti, *Milano*
marcodellatorre.studio
Happy Happy

Nuova Accademia Belle Arti, *Milano*
marcodellatorre.studio
Happy Happy, Lola

LUCEPLAN SPA
Via E.T. Moneta, 40
20161 Milano
T +39 02 662421
F +39 02 66203400
N. verde 800 800 169
info@luceplan.com

LUCEPLAN USA
26 Broadway
NY 10004 New York
T +1 212 98.96.265
F +1 212 46.24.349
info@luceplanusa.com

LUCEPLAN SCANDINAVIA
Klubiensvej 22
Pakhus 48 - Frihavnen
DK 2100 Copenaghen
T +45 36.13.21.00
F +45 36.13.21.01
info@luceplan.net

LUCEPLAN FRANCE
7, Impasse Charles Petit
F-75011 Paris
T +33 1 44.83.92.87
F +33 1 44.83.92.88
luceplan_fr@luceplan.com

LUCEPLAN GERMANY
Prenzlauer Allee 39
D-10405 Berlin
T +49 30 44.33.84.0
F +49 30 44.33.84.22
luceplan_de@luceplan.com

LUCEPLAN STORES

MILANO
Corso Monforte 7
20122 Milano
T +39 02 76015760
F +39 02 784062
luceplanstore@luceplan.com

NEW YORK
47-49 Greene Street
NY 10013 New York
T +1 212 966 1399
F +1 212 966 1799
info@luceplanusa.com

PARIS
225 Rue Fbg Saint Honoré
75008 Paris
T +33 (0) 146222152
F +33 (0) 146689673
luceplan_fr@luceplan.com

www.luceplan.com
www.elementi.luceplan.com